OUR COUNTRY

GERMANY

Written and photographed by

David Cumming

Wayland

Our Country

Australia
Canada
China
France
Germany
Greece
India
Italy
Jamaica
Japan
The Netherlands
New Zealand
Pakistan
Russia
Spain
The United Kingdom
The United States

Cover *The River Danube at Passau in southern Germany*

Series editor: Rosemary Ashley
Book editor: Joanne Jessop
Designer: Jenny Hughes

First published in 1993 by
Wayland (Publishers) Ltd
61 Western Road, Hove
East Sussex BN3 1JD, England

© Copyright 1993 Wayland (Publishers) Ltd

British Library Cataloguing in Publication Data
Cumming, David
  Germany. – (Our Country Series)
  I. Title II. Series
  943.087

  ISBN 0-7502-0850-3

Typeset by Dorchester Typesetting Group Ltd
Printed and bound in Italy by Rotolito Lombarda S.p.A.

All words printed in **bold** are explained in the glossary on page 30.

Contents

We live in Germany	4
The weather	6
Farming	8
Industry and jobs	10
Schools	12
Religion	14
Festivals	16
Homes	18
Sports and pastimes	20
Food	22
Shopping	24
Transport	26
Let's discuss Germany	28
Glossary	30
Books to read	31
Index	32

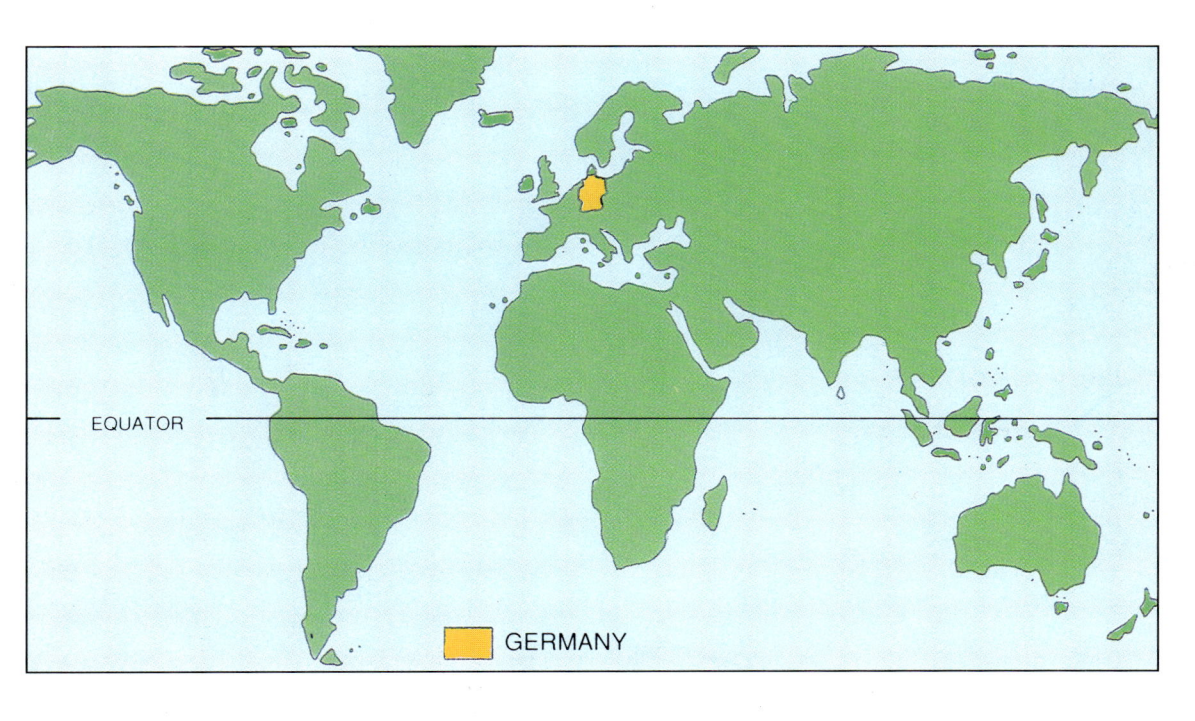

We live in Germany

A village in the hilly countryside of central Germany.

Germany is in the middle of Europe. The land is flat in the north, hilly in the centre and there are mountains in the far south.

When the **Second World War** ended in 1945, Germany was divided into East and West Germany. East Germany had a **Communist government** and East Germans had less freedom and a lower **standard of living** than West Germans. The people of East Germany became unhappy about the way their country was being run, so they changed their government. In 1990, East and West Germany joined together as one country with a **democratic government**.

In this book, twelve children from all over Germany tell you about their lives.

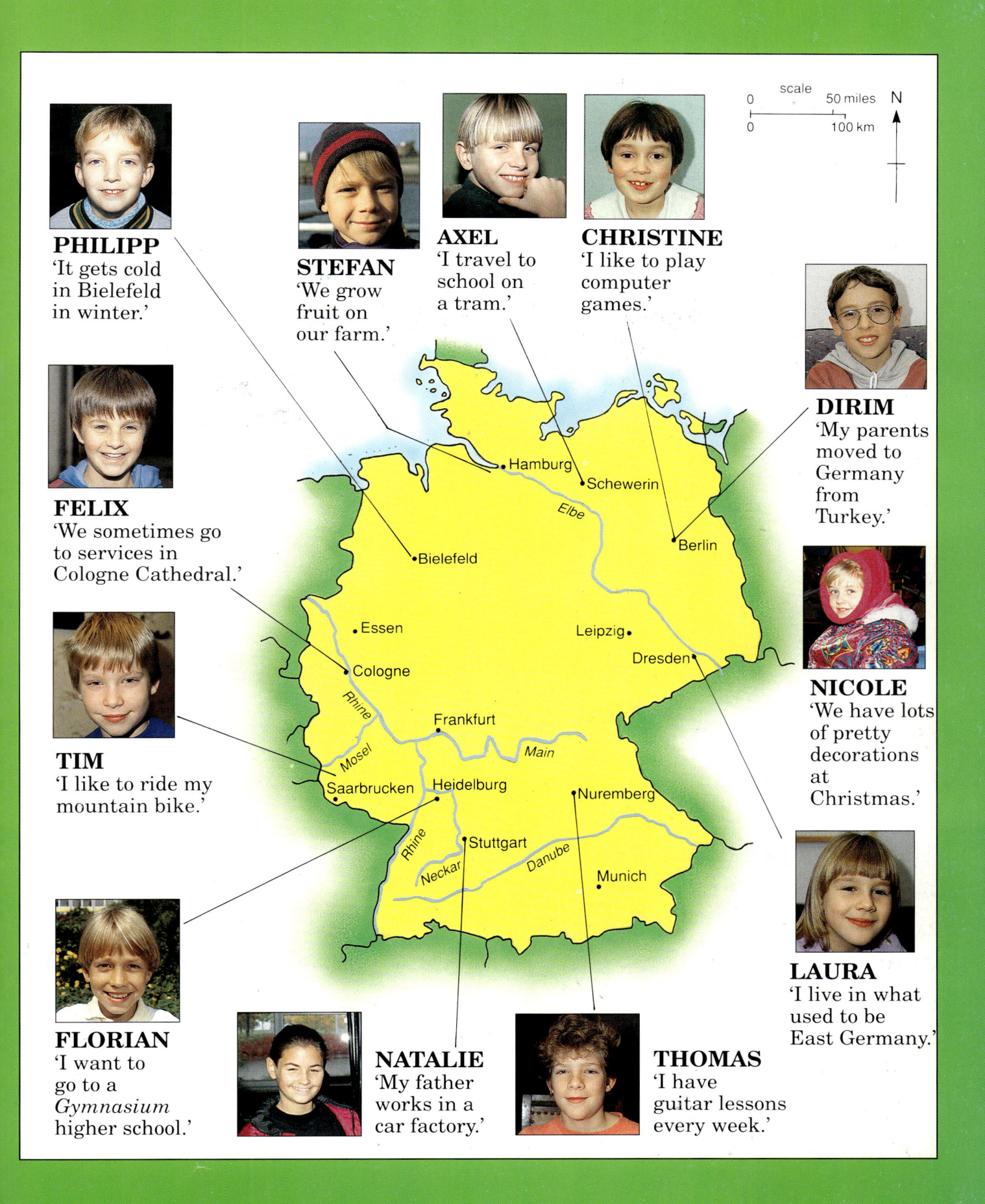

PHILIPP
'It gets cold in Bielefeld in winter.'

STEFAN
'We grow fruit on our farm.'

AXEL
'I travel to school on a tram.'

CHRISTINE
'I like to play computer games.'

DIRIM
'My parents moved to Germany from Turkey.'

FELIX
'We sometimes go to services in Cologne Cathedral.'

TIM
'I like to ride my mountain bike.'

NICOLE
'We have lots of pretty decorations at Christmas.'

FLORIAN
'I want to go to a *Gymnasium* higher school.'

NATALIE
'My father works in a car factory.'

THOMAS
'I have guitar lessons every week.'

LAURA
'I live in what used to be East Germany.'

scale
0   50 miles
0   100 km
N

Hamburg
Schewerin
Elbe
Bielefeld
Berlin
Essen
Leipzig
Cologne
Dresden
Rhine
Frankfurt
Mosel
Main
Saarbrucken
Heidelburg
Nuremberg
Rhine
Stuttgart
Neckar
Danube
Munich

The weather

Northern Germany is near the sea, so the weather there does not get too cold in winter or too hot in summer. Even so, people have to wrap up warmly in winter, and in summer it is hot enough to sunbathe on the beaches of the North Sea and the Baltic Sea.

The southern part of Germany is further from the sea, so here the winters are colder and the summers are hotter than in the north. In winter there is enough snow for

A hot summer's day – perfect weather for sailing a boat on Lake Walchen in southern Germany.

sledging and skiing in the **Alps**. In summer the rivers and lakes of southern Germany are full of people swimming and sailing.

'In summer we play outside in the sun.'

'I am Florian, and I live in Heidelberg, in the south of Germany. During the summer we often play outside because the weather is sunny and hot. Here I am playing leapfrog with my friends. In winter it gets very cold and rains a lot. Sometimes it snows and we have snowball fights.'

'We need to wear warm clothes in winter.'

'My name is Philipp, and I live in Bielefeld, in the north. We wear warm clothes in winter because it gets very cold, especially when it's windy. In this picture I am visiting an outdoor museum of old buildings with my class. I am in the front, in the grey jacket. The houses in the museum had no central heating – people must have frozen in winter!'

Farming

Almost half of the land in Germany is used for growing **crops** or for **grazing** animals.

The most important crops are sugar beet, barley, wheat and sweet corn. In the south, grapes are grown to make wine. The best wines come from grapes that grow on the hills along the River Rhine and the smaller rivers that flow into it.

Grapes growing in vineyards on the slopes above the River Rhine.

'This is the biggest fruit-growing area in all of Germany.'

'My name is Stefan, and I live on a farm near Hamburg. These are some of our apple trees. We also grow pears, strawberries, cherries, plums and raspberries. This is the biggest area for growing fruit in Germany.'

'The Romans were the first to make wine here.'

'I am Laura, and I am helping my mother with the shopping. She is buying some bottles of German wine. She says the Romans were the first to make wine here. Most of the grapes for wine are grown in the south, along the steep sides of the Rhine, Neckar and Mosel rivers.'

In the **foothills** of the Alps and the flat land of the north, farmers keep cattle for their meat and milk. Many farmers also raise chickens, sheep and pigs, which they also sell for their meat.

Industry and jobs

Germany's **industries** are the third most important in the world, after those of the USA and Japan. Out of every 100 workers in Germany, 41 have jobs in factories.

German industries include making cars, machinery, **chemicals**, **household appliances** and electrical goods such as televisions, video recorders and computers. Many of these products are sold to other countries, especially to other European countries.

Many industries in what used to be East Germany are trying to catch up with the more modern industries in the western part of the country. But some factories in the east

Ship repairing is an important industry in the port of Hamburg.

are so old and out of date that they are being shut down, and many workers are losing their jobs.

'The car industry is the biggest industry in Germany.'

'I am Natalie, and here I am with my father in the Mercedes car factory where he works. We are looking at the engine of a car that is nearly finished. The car industry is the biggest industry in Germany, and Mercedes is one of the most important motor companies.'

'All Germans can run their own businesses now.'

'My name is Axel, and I live in Schwerin, in what used to be East Germany. Here I am in the office of my parents' business. They print all sorts of things, from invitations to adverts. In East Germany this would not have been possible because most businesses were owned by the government. But nowadays all Germans can run their own businesses.'

Schools

Most children go to a kindergarten for a year or two before they start school at the age of six. The school-day begins at 8 o'clock in the morning and finishes at lunchtime, with a break at about 10.30 in the morning for a snack.

In every school, girls and boys study together, and no one wears a uniform.

Almost all schools are run by the government, so parents pay no fees. There is a long holiday in the summer and there are shorter ones at Christmas and Easter, as well as half-term breaks.

Children in a classroom of a Berlin school. The school is in the part of Berlin that used to be in East Germany.

At the age of ten, children leave their primary school and go to a high school, where the school-day is longer and the work is harder.

'We get more and more homework as we grow older.'

'My name is Thomas. Here I am sitting at the desk in my bedroom, doing my geography homework. When we first go to school we don't have much homework, but we get more and more as we grow older! I try to do it when I get home, early in the afternoon.'

'I want to go to a *Gymnasium*.'

'I am Florian, and here I am with my class in the school playground. I am on the left in the Mickey Mouse sweat shirt. I am good at my lessons, so when I leave I want to go to a *Gymnasium* higher school. When I am 18 years old, I can take exams to go to university.'

13

Religion

A statue of the Virgin Mary with Jesus. It is in southern Germany where many of the people are Roman Catholic.

Germany is a **Christian** country, with more **Protestants** than **Roman Catholics**. There are 46 million Protestants and 35 million Catholics in Germany. Most Protestants live in the north and the east, and most Catholics live in the south.

In the countryside there are still a few villages where the churches are full, but many Christians in Germany do not go to church very often.

Many people from other countries have come to live and work in Germany, and they have brought their own religions with them. The most common religion among these new

'My parents came here from Turkey and we are Muslims.'

'I am Dirim, and I live in Berlin. My parents come from Turkey. They moved here to work in 1980 and I was born three years later. We are Muslims, which means that we practise the religion of Islam. This is one of the mosques that has been built for Muslims in Berlin.'

'Cologne Cathedral is the biggest cathedral in Germany.'

'My name is Felix, and I live near Cologne. We sometimes go to services in Cologne's **cathedral** because they are special. The cathedral is the most important Protestant church in Germany, as well as the biggest.'

Germans is **Islam**, whose followers are called Muslims. About 2 million Muslims now live in Germany. Many **mosques** have been built where Muslims go to pray.

15

Festivals

Since most Germans are Christians, the important religious festivals are Christian holy days. Germans are famous for their Christmas celebrations. At Christmas time, there are special markets and fun-fairs. City streets sparkle with colourful lights, and homes are full of pretty decorations.

People of other religions also celebrate their own holy days, with many Christians joining in.

Children with their lanterns at the festival for St Martin in Dusseldorf, in northern Germany.

'All our streets and homes are decorated for Christmas.'

'I am Nicole. I have just bought this cuddly Father Christmas doll at the market which is held in our town every year just before Christmas. All our streets and homes are decorated at Christmas time.'

'I always have a big birthday party.'

'I am Felix, and this is what I hope to get for my birthday! Building model cars is fun, so I have asked my parents to buy me this one for my collection. I always have a big birthday party and invite all my friends round to my home.'

There are also festivals all over Germany to mark the change in seasons. The biggest one is Carnival, which is held at the end of winter. There are big parades of people in fancy dress in many cities. In autumn, there are wine and beer festivals to celebrate the season's **harvest**.

Homes

Old and new houses in a village in southern Germany.

More Germans live in large towns and cities than in villages or in the countryside. Homes are usually flats, not houses. Many of the flats in eastern Germany are not as comfortable as those in the west, but housing in the east is being improved.

Homes in the cities and towns tend to look the same all over Germany; but houses in the villages change from area to area. In the south, for example, houses have high roofs so that the snow slides off easily in winter.

Most families do not own their homes because they are very expensive. Instead they **rent** them from the government or from someone else.

Germans are very proud of their homes, so they try to buy the best of everything for them. Their homes are kept neat and tidy, and the furniture and household appliances are usually very modern.

'We live in a flat like most city families in Germany.'

'I am Dirim, and my home is in Berlin, the **capital** of Germany. We live in a comfortable modern flat. This is the unit in my room. The top is a bed, and underneath there is a desk and cupboard and shelves for storing my things. It helps me to keep the room tidy, which pleases my mum and dad!'

'I live in a village in south-west Germany.'

'My name is Tim, and I live in a house in a village in the south-west of Germany. This is the playroom my father built for me in the attic. There is also a bedroom on the same floor, so I have lots of space. Most people rent their homes, but my parents own this house.'

Sports and pastimes

Sports are very popular in Germany. About one person in four belongs to a sports club, and many Germans play sports without being club members. So it is not surprising that so many world champions in all kinds of sports have come from Germany.

Football is the most popular team sport. Thousands of fans turn up every week to watch clubs such as Bayern Munich and Dynamo Dresden in action. The German national team won the World Cup in 1990.

In winter, many Germans go skiing in the mountains. In summer, they like to go

A swimming race on the River Neckar at Heidelberg.

'When this was East Germany it was difficult to buy computer games.'

'I am Christine, and I like playing computer games with my friend. The part of Berlin where I live used to be in East Germany, and it was difficult to buy computer games. Since Germany has become one country again many shops sell computer games. I did not have any games before, but now I have lots.'

'I taught myself to play the classical guitar.'

'My name is Thomas, and I have taught myself to play the classical guitar. I also have lessons every week to help me improve. I would like to buy an electric guitar, but my parents say I would make too much noise!'

walking and cycling in the hills and forests. Many Germans travel to other countries during their holidays, often with their own tents or caravans.

Food

Germans leave home early for work and school, so breakfast is a roll with butter and jam or a bowl of cereal. Adults have a cup of coffee, and children have a milky drink.

Lunch is the main meal of the day, and the evening supper is a cold snack with a selection of meats, cheese and sausages.

Germany is famous for its sausages, and many different kinds are made. Most sausages can be bought everywhere, but some are special to an area or city. For example, frankfurters come from the city of Frankfurt. Some shops sell nothing but sausages.

A sausage stall selling many types of sausages.

'I love pizzas and Indian and Chinese food.'

'I am Axel. Here I am enjoying an indoor barbecue. We are cooking small pieces of steak, pork and mushrooms on an electric hot plate, then dipping them in sauces. Last night we had an Italian pizza. There are also takeaways where you can get Indian and Chinese food.'

'On most streets you can buy snacks like this.'

'My name is Stefan. I am eating a snack while I am out for the day. It is a *Frikadelle*, which is minced meat in breadcrumbs, in a crusty roll. On most streets you can buy snacks like this from stalls that also sell sausages, hamburgers and chips.'

People who have moved to Germany have opened up restaurants and shops that sell food from the countries they have come from. Many Germans now enjoy foods such as pizzas and kebabs as well as traditional German dishes.

Shopping

The traffic-free shopping area in the centre of Stuttgart.

To buy some things such as shoes, clothes or toys, people go to the large **department stores** in the centre of towns and cities. Shopping here is more enjoyable now that cars are not allowed in the city centres.

Once a week, many people drive to the new **hypermarkets** outside the cities to stock up on everyday things for the home.

Every week, too, many Germans go to their nearest outdoor market to buy fresh fruit and vegetables from the farmers.

By law, all shops and markets must close at lunchtime on Saturdays so that people can have a long weekend. However, on the first Saturday of each month and near Christmas, shops and markets can stay

'Shops have many more things since Germany became one country again.'

'My name is Laura, and I live in what used to be East Germany. There are many more things in the shops since Germany became one country again. Also, things that were very expensive are now much cheaper. Here I am with my mother in a supermarket. It is difficult to know what to buy, there is so much choice.'

'I am allowed to test the new computer games.'

'I am Christine, and I am in my favourite shop in Berlin. It sells all sorts of electrical things. I come here to buy my computer games because I am allowed to test the new ones to see what they are like. In the old East Germany there were no shops like this one.'

open until 6.00 pm. On Thursdays shops stay open until 8.00 pm so that people can shop after work.

Transport

It is quick and easy to travel between the big cities in Germany by land, using the roads and railways, and by air, on one of the many plane services.

Many goods, especially big and bulky things, are carried to and from factories on **barges**. The barges travel along the rivers and **canals**, taking goods all over Germany as well as to nearby countries.

Germans like to drive everywhere, so a family often has two cars. With so many cars, there are traffic jams, **pollution** and parking problems. The government is trying

The River Rhine is the most important river in Germany for the transport of goods.

to solve these problems by making people leave their cars outside cities and by making it more expensive to own a car.

'I catch the tram to school in term-time.'

'My name is Axel, and I catch the **tram** to school. In winter, it is still dark in the morning when I get on the tram. Children can buy special tickets and passes that are cheaper than anyone else's. Trams are much faster than cars or buses because they are not held up in traffic jams.'

'It is quite usual to see whole families out on their bikes.'

'My name is Tim. I like riding my mountain bike, even on cold, dull days like today. Cycling is very popular in Germany, and you often see whole families out on their bikes. We are very lucky because there are cycle paths everywhere now. There is a cycle route along the River Danube that is over 200 km long. One day I will do it!'

Let's discuss Germany

This book has told you a little about Germany and the lives of some children who live there. If you could travel to Germany, which part of the country would you most like to see? Why? If you lived in Germany, would you like to live on a farm like Stefan or in a big city such as Berlin, where Dirim and Christine live?

In what ways is Germany like your country? Are there forests and mountains in your country? Does it snow in winter, where you live, so you can have snowball fights like Florian and his friends? Do you have some of the same holidays as Germans?

Facts

Population:
 80 million
Capital: Berlin
Language:
 German
Money:
 German mark
Religion: Mainly Protestant and Roman Catholic

People come from all over the world to visit the beautiful city of Heidelberg.

Do you have Christmas decorations like Nicole's family? How is your school different from the schools in Germany?

What do you think children from Germany would find different or strange if they came to visit your country? What would be the same?

This is the Brandenburg Gate, a famous landmark in Berlin.

There are many beautiful castles in Germany. This one overlooks the River Rhine.

Glossary

Alps The mountain range in central Europe that runs through parts of France, Italy, Switzerland, Austria and southern Germany.

Barges Flat-bottomed boats used on canals and rivers.

Canals Artificial rivers that are built for boats and small ships to travel along.

Capital The most important city of a country and the centre of its government.

Cathedral A large and important church.

Chemicals Substances made by a chemical process. These can include medicines, face creams, paints and plastics.

Christian Having to do with Christianity, the religion based on the teachings of Jesus Christ. People who follow Christianity are known as Christians.

Communist government A government under which all industry and commerce is owned by the state and there is no private property.

Crops Plants such as wheat and corn that are grown by farmers for food.

Democratic government A government that is elected by the people of the country.

Department store A big store that sells many different products.

Foothills The smaller hills that surround a group of higher mountains.

Grazing The feeding or raising of cattle.

Harvest Crops that have ripened and been picked.

Household appliances Machines used to do tasks in the house, such as ovens, washing machines and vacuum cleaners.

Hypermarket A very large supermarket outside a town or city.

Industry The manufacture of goods, such as cars, clothing and chemicals.

Islam The religion based on the teachings of the Prophet Muhammad. The followers of Islam are known as Muslims.

Mosque A holy building in which Muslims pray.

Pollution Dirt or poisons in the air, water or ground.

Protestants Members of branches of the Christian Church other than Roman Catholic or Greek or Russian Orthodox.

Rent To pay money for using something that belongs to another person.

Roman Catholics Members of the Roman Catholic Church, which is a branch of Christianity headed by the Pope in Rome.
Second World War The war that started in 1939 when Germany attacked Poland. The war ended in 1945 when Britain, France, the USA and the USSR defeated Germany.
Standard of living The way in which people live and the kind of goods they can afford to buy.
Tram A passenger vehicle similar to a bus, which runs on rails through city streets.

Books to read

German Family by Ann Adler (A & C Black, 1984)

Germany, People and Places series (Macmillan, 1989)

West Germany Is My Country by Bernice and Cliff Moon (Wayland, 1985)

Germany (Countries of the World) by David Cumming (Wayland, 1993)

Acknowledgements

The author would like to thank all the families who helped in the production of this book, as well as Ursula Rudrum, Thomas Lernbecher, and Günter, Gisela and Tanja Nause.

Picture acknowledgements

All photographs are by David Cumming except for the following: pages 15 (top) and 29 (top) by Zefa. The maps on contents page and page 5 are by Jenny Hughes.

Index

Alps **6, 9, 30**
Australia **11**

Baltic Sea **6**
Bayern Munich **20**
Berlin **12, 15, 19, 21, 24, 28, 29**
Bielefeld **7**
Brandenburg Gate **29**

canals **26, 30**
Carnival **17**
cars **10, 11, 26–7**
Christians **16, 30**
Christmas **12, 16, 17, 24, 29**
Cologne **15**
Cologne Cathedral **15**
Communist government **4, 30**

Danube, River **27**
Dusseldorf **16**
Dynamo Dresden **20**

East Germany **4, 10, 11, 12, 21, 25**
Easter **12**
Europe **4, 10**

factories **10, 26**
farming **8–9**
festivals **16–17**
flats **18, 19**
food **22–3**
football **20**
Frankfurt **22**
frankfurter **22**
Frikadelle **23**

Gymnasium **13**

Hamburg **9, 10**
Heidelberg **7, 20, 28**
holidays **12, 21, 28**
homes **18–19**
hypermarkets **24, 30**

industry **10–11, 30**
Islam **14, 30**

jobs **10–11**

kindergarten **12**

markets **16, 17, 24**
Mosel, River **9**
mosques **14, 15, 30**
Muslims **14, 15**

Neckar, River **9, 20**
North Sea **6**

pastimes **20–21**
pollution **26, 30**
Protestants **14, 28, 30**

religion **14–15, 16**
Rhine, River **8, 9, 26, 29**
Roman Catholics **14, 28, 30**

sausages **22**
schools **12–13, 29**
Schwerin **11**
Second World War **4, 31**
shopping **24–5**
sports **6, 20–21**
Stuttgart **24**

traffic **26, 27**
trams **27, 31**
transport **26–7**
Turkey **15**

Walchen, Lake **6**
weather **6–7**
West Germany **4**
wine **8, 9**
World Cup **20**